GW00731924

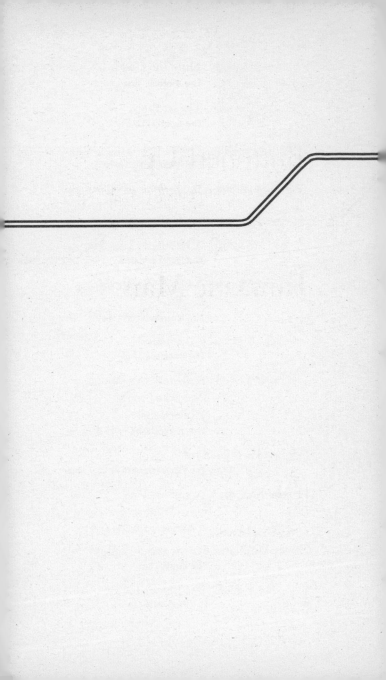

Buttoned-Up

A survey of a curious fashion phenomenon

Fantastic Man

PENGUIN BOOKS

PENGUIN BOOKS

Published by the Penguin Group

Penguin Books Ltd, 80 Strand, London WC2R 0RL, England

Penguin Group (USA) Inc., 375 Hudson Street, New York, New York 10014, USA

Penguin Group (Canada), 90 Eglinton Avenue East, Suite 700, Toronto, Ontario, Canada
M4P 2Y3 (a division of Pearson Penguin Canada Inc.)

Penguin Ireland, 25 St Stephen's Green, Dublin 2, Ireland (a division of Penguin Books Ltd)

Penguin Group (Australia), 250 Camberwell Road, Camberwell, Victoria 3124, Australia
(a division of Pearson Australia Group Pty Ltd)

Penguin Books India Pvt Ltd, 11 Community Centre, Panchsheel Park, New Delhi – 110 017,

India Penguin Group (NZ), 67 Apollo Drive, Rosedale, Auckland 0632, New Zealand
(a division of Pearson New Zealand Ltd)

Penguin Books (South Africa) (Pty) Ltd, Block D, Rosebank Office Park, 181 Jan Smuts
Avenue, Parktown North, Gauteng 2193, South Africa

Penguin Books Ltd, Registered Offices: 80 Strand, London WC2R 0RL, England

www.penguin.com

First published in Penguin Books 2013
001

Selection and editorial material copyright © Superlandia BV, 2013

The moral right of the editors has been asserted

Set in Baskerville MT Std 11.75/15pt
Typeset by Claire Mason
Printed in Great Britain by Clays Ltd, St Ives plc

A CIP catalogue record for this book is available from the British Library

ISBN: 978-1-846-14568-1

www.greenpenguin.co.uk

ALWAYS LEARNING   PEARSON

Dedicated to mankind

Contents

East End
Six junctions photographed in East London,
by Andrew T. Vottero, on pages: 1–2, 3–4, 31–32,
33–34, 105–106, 107–108

East End

Street corners along the East London Line,
photographed by Andrew T. Vottero

Junction No. 1:
Fleur De Lis Street and Blossom Street, E1

Junction No. 2:
Tabernacle Street and Plantina Street, EC2A

Here, and on the cover, 25-year-old Giordano Cioni, a production manager living in East London. Photograph by Benjamin Alexander Huseby.

Buttoned-Up

The editors of *Fantastic Man* explore a curious
fashion phenomenon

When departing the East London Line at
Shoreditch High Street, one might choose to
visit one of the several fashionable menswear
retailers that thrive in the Borough of Hackney.
It is likely that one will notice a distinct
similarity in the way these shop's employees and
customers have dressed themselves: they'll be
wearing their shirts with the buttons done up
all the way to the top, the collars closed tight
around their necks. This approach to dressing is
not the most comfortable one by any means, but
in this area of London and many other corners
of modern society it is miraculously popular.

Buttoned-up has become the norm.

The simple act of fastening a shirt's highest button and the plainness of the look it creates belies a variety of intricate and complex intentions. It presents an appearance that is at once proper in its neatness and rebellious in the deliberate exclusion of a tie. Buttoning up stakes a particular territory for its wearer, especially in East London, an area famed for its creative industry. It suggests something puritanical, an almost Amish eschewing of decoration, a refusal to reveal anything below the neck. It infantilizes, recalling images of first days of school and boys being dressed by their mothers. It is an up-tight look dating back to the restrained aggression of the mod sixties. It is virtually unavoidable in menswear fashion imagery, where it easily provides a sense of considered smartness. Buttoning up is contemporary but timeless.

The following pages present an attempt to understand the look's basis in fashion, history and pop culture – what motivates men to expose themselves to the discomforts and delights of buttoning up.

Gert Jonkers & Jop van Bennekom,
editors of *Fantastic Man*

White cotton shirt, photographed by Maurice Scheltens and
Liesbeth Abbenes for *Fantastic Man* No.5, 2007.

To Button Up

Why men in East London dress the way they do,
by Paul Flynn

Patrick's school uniform in rural Scotland was
a white shirt and V-neck jumper, no tie. He says
the boys would wear their shirts one button open
and the girls maybe one more. Just teenagers,
loosening up. When he was sixteen he happened
upon a picture in a magazine of Orange Juice
guitarist James Kirk. 'He was holding his guitar
and he had a really long trench coat and a bowl
cut,' says Patrick. 'He had his shirt buttoned
up. I thought he looked like the coolest person
in the world.' Prompted by this revelation,
Patrick decided in a small moment of schoolboy
rebellion to follow his lead.

This was his first personal styling decision, inspired by a whimsical Glasgow pop group nobody could guess the reach of at the time. Orange Juice's deftly amateurish fusing of black groove with white noise, not to mention their charity-shop chic, would set a template for the future sound and look of bands who were interested in any of the crossover points on the tangent between wee small hours disco and college rock.

Whenever he buttoned up like James Kirk, Patrick felt nice. 'At school I thought I was a lot cooler than everyone else.' Given his unusual key visual references – he also mentions The Go-Betweens and The Jesus and Mary Chain – he probably was. 'I guess it was my way of asserting difference.'

Last summer, I wandered with my brother Peter up the regulation East End pathway, from Whitechapel through Columbia Road, on to Hackney Road, winding through back-street Haggerston estates through to Kingsland Road and ending up in Dalston. My brother was of the age and inclination to listen to those musicians in his bedroom and watch them play the first time round. We stopped and took the temperature of this strictly self-regulated new Metropolitan runway. A lot of boys looked like they might've had their lives changed by a picture of a pasty '80s musician. 'Everyone looks like they are going to Devilles,' Peter suggested.

Devilles was one of a small selection of Manchester nightclubs in the early to mid-'80s that housed an angsty, interior youth subset that would peak and swiftly implode after the *NME* magazine *C86* compilation dropped. It smelt of Breaker lager, Benson & Hedges cigarettes and early adult anxiety. The DJ sported a quiff just like Tintin. The patrons of Devilles coupled a bracing Northern humour born out of boredom with poetically abject thought. The soundtrack of this mating ground was winsome independent rock and New York City street funk, tied together only by sharing the noisy distinction of being made on a shoestring budget. It was one of those places that was driven by teenage difference; whose visual undercurrent said 'we might not have as much money as you but we have got better ideas,' cocking a snook at the emerging, blousy wine-bar scene in the city. Everyone in Devilles in 1985 was buttoned up.

Almost three decades later, Patrick is one of those faces that you find dotted about the East End, who brightens the social landscape with a similar dismissal for corporate culture to folks in '80s Manchester. He shares more with his native predecessors in Scotland and the North of England than a penchant for fastening his shirt at the collar, that wilful style act of self-strangulation. He is the drummer in a band called Veronica Falls who continue the emotional lineage of matching cheap music to exquisite thought. It is a band that leaves the tendons of its intention exposed and unpolished. Patrick gives off the primary air of not giving a fuck whether Veronica Falls makes a penny from what they are doing beyond funding the next night out. He has served counter shifts at the amusingly diffident pub the Nelson's Head, housed behind the Costcutter on Hackney Road, to make rent between tours. Veronica Falls will never be Coldplay in the way Orange Juice would never be U2. Some people don't want that.

He always buttons up on stage; a nod to his ramshackle heroes and forebears. 'If I ever see a picture of myself playing, and for some reason I've unbuttoned my top button, I always feel a bit angry at myself,' he says, 'I feel it makes a big difference to the way you wear a shirt. It's really subtle but it changes an entire outfit. If I'm not buttoned up it feels a bit like something's missing, like I've not finished getting dressed.'

Once, on a date, someone asked Patrick to unbutton his shirt. 'I remember being shocked because I didn't even think of it as being weird. They made a comment about me trying to give off the impression that I was unobtainable, or really strait-laced.'

And did he honour the request?

'No.'

...

The Nelson's Head sits at the almost exact midway point between the Pride of Spitalfields and the Shacklewell Arms, the two pubs that are the most obvious outer map points of buttoned-up London. It is a marvellous place, its buttoned-up customers a fractious and brilliantly divisive reminder that the wheels of the countercultural bus set in stone in the '80s – at that fascinating, intensely style-conscious time post punk and pre acid house – not only refuse to stop turning but can also career toward reckless, drunken fun.

This subset of buttoned-up London has not quite been nailed and taken into mainstream dialogue, apart from some mocking in *Vice* magazine's online drama *Dalston Superstars* and on the comically accurate website *East London Gays*. But nobody has sincerely explored why it is that boys who feel different from other boys ended up on the Brick Lane/Stoke Newington strip of decrepit, anti-corporate night-time culture and, moreover, ended up wearing their shirts buttoned up to inhabit it.

Some of it must be a reaction to the

predominant suburban neck-line of the reality TV generation: the deep-V-necked T-shirt favoured by boyband stylists and body obsessives. The man in a deep V is open, ready, disposable. The buttoned-up man has a flavour of some entrenched, considered mystery. We would've once considered him pretentious, if preferring books to TV can be adjudged as such. He does not favour the more expositional approach to male sex-appeal in his wardrobe.

'I think there's something sexy in people taking the time to consider their appearance,' says Josh, a thirty-year-old button-up devotee from Dalston. 'I don't think you would accidentally walk around with your top button done up and no tie. It's all the little details.'

Stephen is twenty-seven, lives in Bethnal Green, and always buttons his shirt up, despite it drawing attention to a part of his body he feels slightly awkward with. 'I have quite a fat neck,' he says flatly. But he finds buttoning up a satisfying way of dealing with another body issue, his hirsuteness. 'I'm quite hairy, and I always had my chest hair on show.' He began buttoning up two years ago. 'When you're hairy you tend to always look a bit scruffy, and I wanted to show a different side of me. It also looks quite neat.' He says buttoning up is not a sexual statement, before reconsidering, 'maybe, but that wasn't really in my mind when I was doing it. There is a sort of uniformness about it. It's like a school uniform for adults.'

'I feel more attractive personally when I do it,' says Sam, an artist from the East End, of his decision to button up. 'It is quite sexy. Look at it this way – if one more button is done up, then that's one more button that has to be undone. If somebody's done-up, then there's going to be a certain amount of undoing to do, in a good way. There's more left to the imagination. For instance, if someone's wearing a belt then you can't just whip their trousers off – you have to get the belt off first.'

There is a simple, architectural fashion angle to buttoning up. 'I think this looks more refined,' says Sam, purposefully separating himself from the neighbourhood bar scruffs. 'It's just something that I've always known to be smart. It looks a lot smoother, it accentuates the neck and the face in a much better way and also it accentuates the shirt itself.' There is history to it. 'You know, Edwardian gentlemen who would wear a tailcoat and a stiff collar? A squared-off collar, where you steam the corners. I would say what I do is a modern take on that.' There is economy, too. 'Part of the nicest thing about it is that you don't have to buy something new,' says Stephen, 'you can just wear something in your wardrobe in a different way.'

'There's been a bit of a return to traditional styling, but slightly nuanced,' says Josh. 'You do see people who are buttoning their collars or who are wearing a decent tweed jacket. There's more of an emphasis, in the same way that men's grooming took off after a while. It's a natural progression that once they've sorted the grooming out, they're not going to want to wear a suit from Burton with some horrible open-neck collar or estate-agent tie.'

The problem with a point of difference when it comes to personal presentation is that once a lot of people who feel different congregate in a small area, all sporting their difference together, it becomes normalized. It is not different anymore. It is the same.

Buttoning up feels like not just a recognizably Metropolitan styling tic but a recognizably East End move, as postcode-defining as the jumper over the shoulders is to the Putney and Fulham public-school set at the capital's other economic extreme in the West, or wearing one's hood up is in South London. Anyone exposed to the provincial geographical style-markings of the London boroughs will identify buttoning up as an East thing. This is the menswear language I see every day in the square two miles circumnavigating my home.

The self-consciously thought-through pubs of Hackney and Tower Hamlets, with their junk-shop decor and continuing investigation into the aesthetics of the wrong are dotted with compelling top-button wearers. Though one might expect buttoning up to be encouraged in the defining industries of the area that trade off their point of difference – fashion, design, art, music, advertising, outré bar and restaurant

Text continues on page 28

Boys
by Benjamin Alexander Huseby

Joshua Aberhart, 22,
works as a costume
designer and pastry chef.

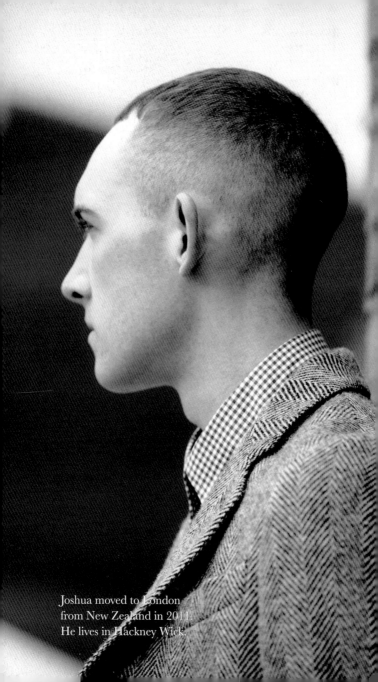

Joshua moved to London
from New Zealand in 2011.
He lives in Hackney Wick.

Moses Manley works as an umbrella maker. The 23-year-old lives in East London along the Regent's Canal.

25-year-old Owen Myers
moved to London to pursue a
career in jounalism. He lives
in Dalston.

Abel Llavall-Ubach, 26, works
as a film production assistant.

Abel was born in Paris, France, and has resided in London since 2010.

22-year-old Matthew Vant is
a songwriter and filmmaker
living in Dalston, East London.

Jasper Toron Nielsen, 32, is a menswear designer who moved to London from Copenhagen ten years ago.

cultures – it still comes as a mild shock to hear that Josh, the thirty-year-old from Dalston, wears his East End outfit (healthy beard, groomed moustache, trousers half an inch too short, lustrous hair side-parted, shirt buttoned up) to work at as a legal support at a City law firm.

The City is still slave to Savile Row tailoring; they button up only to facilitate a tie. Josh calls his work look 'business casual', but he's quite alone in taking a suggestion of the bar-hopping menswear traits of the East into the neighbouring financial sector.

'In that kind of conservative environment,' he says, 'it's easy to fade into the background, and it only takes a few subtle nuances to have people spot that you're not doing what they're doing. I have a reputation across the firm. People that I don't know know who I am and often comment on the fact that I don't wear a tie. It's a bit weird. They say, "Oh right, you must be a creative, then." I dread to think what nicknames they've given me! Buttoning up is one of the things that keep me sane when working in that environment! You look at history, you look at mods, and you'd have guys working in the post room that were wearing better suits than the manager of the company. It's just using clothing as an expression of distaste of a system that you have to be involved with, for whatever reason. The small victories that you can gain by buttoning your shirt differently... '

If at work he is setting a new agenda with his approach to office wear, Josh is happy to admit that socially, whilst slipping between East End hostelries, he was following a noticeable local pattern when he started to button up. 'I'd seen it popping up here and there, mostly in magazines and on a few people around here. It felt like it might be a good time to start doing something to make myself look different.'

But if buttoning up is no longer a point of looking different in one specific London area, perhaps it is simply a matter of looking better. Ash is staff at Present, the gentlemanly outfitters on Shoreditch High Street. He began buttoning up ten years ago and still maintains the exemplary nature of what it does to the state of a man's wardrobe. His reason for starting to button up was finding an exciting new brand. 'You know the Japanese brand Haversack? They do these cut-away rounded collars. They're just really old-fashioned. I started wearing them, and they looked nice done-up. From then I just started doing all my shirts up. It feels comfortable and looks good.'

The top-button boys are a useful international indicator. They have their own special significance in identifying when you might be in the right part of town. Looking good can do that, can't it?

Junction No. 3:
Buxton Street and Code Street, E1

Junction No. 4:
Tabernacle Street and Clere Street, EC2A

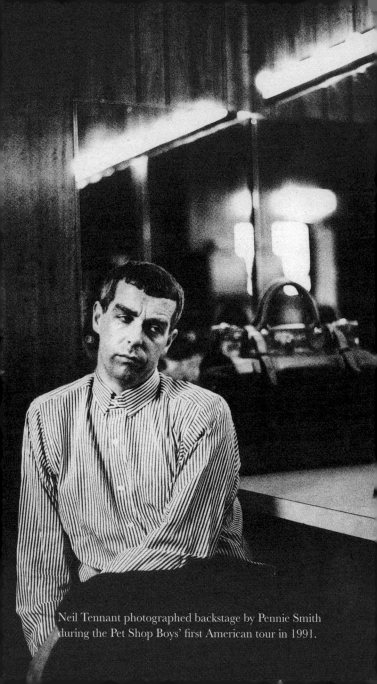

Neil Tennant photographed backstage by Pennie Smith during the Pet Shop Boys' first American tour in 1991.

Quintessentially

Pet Shop Boys' Neil Tennant chats with
Gert Jonkers about his signature look

The Pet Shop Boys are officially Britain's best-
selling pop duo ever. Chris Lowe, who usually
stands behind a keyboard, is a notoriously
sporty dresser, while singer Neil Tennant
maintains a more formal wardrobe. Neil
buttons up his shirts, and wears them
sometimes with, but mostly without, a tie. He
sang about girls in the West End and boys
in the East End on their debut single, 'West
End Girls'. Today, twenty-eight years later,
we're meeting for dinner in a fashionable
East London establishment. Neil is wearing
a buttoned-up white-and-blue Comme des

Garçons shirt under a black denim jacket and dark blue jeans, both by Acne.

GERT JONKERS: You're not from London originally, are you?

NEIL TENNANT: I'm from Newcastle.

GJ: What happened when you came to London? Did you change your look when you came here?

NT: I went to North London Polytechnic in 1972. First term, I lived in the halls of residence, then I got a flat in Tottenham with friends in January 1973. And that's when I cut my hair. I looked so young when I was eighteen, I could get a half-fare on the bus to Newcastle. And when I cut my hair it made me look even younger and I really liked it.

GJ: You cut your hair in 1973? Everybody was still growing long hair in 1973.

NT: I was early. Obviously I then dyed it red.

GJ: Why red?

NT: It was the high point of Bowie! We used to sit in our flat in Tottenham and try on make-up. We were all Bowie fans. I saw the Aladdin Sane tour three times. We used to put Bowie records on and do the moves he did. I used to go to college wearing women's shoes. We had competitions to see who could wear the highest heels. I had these wedge heels. The biggest size you could get was 6.5, but I'm size 8 so I used to walk around with my toes scrunched – quite painful. Isn't it Chinese women who bind their feet? There was an old couple in the flat below us, and they eventually left – their son told me one day that it was the shoes that drove them out, because we were walking around in these wedge heels upstairs. I would listen to *Transformer* by Lou Reed and stomp around the house. I actually felt really bad about it. Still feel bad about it.

GJ: Can you remember the clothes you were wearing at the time?

NT: I had a white tank top that I got from my

mother – this sleeveless knitted top with
a high round neck. You're too young to
remember this, but it was a very tank-toppy
period. I'd wear it over a white shirt,
buttoned up, and white Oxford trousers.

GJ: Why did you button up your shirts?

NT: I like functionality. There's a top button, so
why not use it? Also, an open shirt is just too
casual. It's not me. In fact we once did
a photo session for 'Always On My Mind'
with Pierre La Roche, the famous make-up
artist who did Bowie's Aladdin Sane make-
up, and he forced me to unbutton my shirt.
Chris is wearing a Poshboy hat and we're
both wearing unbelievable amounts of
make-up. I'm being all sexy, wearing a Yohji
Yamamoto shirt open 'til here, a bit of chest
hair… It's pretty rare on me.

GJ: One thing that strikes us very much about
East London is how many young men button
up their shirts all the way to the top.

NT: That is interesting.

GJ: Why do you think they do it? Is it a way of adapting to a new city – like a rite of passage?

NT: I don't know. Also, I've never lived in East London.

GJ: Where did the buttoning up start for you. Did your mother teach you to button up?

NT: Oh no. My mother would have always said, 'Undo the top button.' She always thought I looked a bit too buttoned up. In fact all women will say that. Now that I think of it, I've always had a lot of women come up to me and tell me to undo the top button.

GJ: Do you think you were rebelling against something when you started buttoning up?

NT: Well, yes, I guess I was rebelling against my peers at school. I was rebelling against students in loon pants. Do you know what loon pants are? They're very tight at the crotch with flared legs. I never liked it as a look.

GJ: When you worked at *Smash Hits* later, was

there a specific uniform at the office?

NT: I used to wear Dr. Martens boots and Levi's 501s or the black jeans that Levi's had just launched. All popstars and journalists wore them. And I would wear a checked shirt. Buttoned up.

GJ: That's quite a nice look. How did this evolve into your early Pet Shop Boys looks? I remember it was quite un-popstarry.

NT: Well, you know, we signed to EMI in 1985, which is the year of Live Aid and the height of Duran Duran. We didn't want to be like all that. We wanted to do something dignified; we wanted our image to be based on our personalities, our awkwardness.

GJ: Was that discussed literally – the awkwardness – or did it come naturally?

NT: Naturally. We're quite awkward people, I think. Well, I can't speak for myself, but Chris is quite shy in public.

Chris Lowe, left, and Neil Tennant in a publicity shot from
1986 by Robert Mapplethorpe.

Neil Tennant in a still from the video for 'Paninaro', 1986,
filmed in Milan, Italy, by the Pet Shop Boys themselves.

GJ: Shy? He always looks like a bit of a sex toy in the early Pet Shop Boys photographs.

NT: Chris has a brilliant talent for casual clothes. I remember an issue of *The Face* magazine in 1989 where they had a chart of the one hundred most important people in British fashion – Chris is number three, because he would wear these incredibly expensive Gianfranco Ferré jackets with jeans and trainers... I was always more the problem when it came to looks.

GJ: In the preface of Chris Heath's book *Literally*, from 1990, you refer to your look as 'the school teacher'. Were you okay with that role or was it something that you were somehow forced into?

NT: Totally comfortable with it. I look back on it now and I'm surprised to see how *fashion* the whole thing is. Chris and I never had a stylist. We didn't use stylists until about ten years ago, and even now it just means somebody brings a rack of clothes and we go through it and pick something to wear. In the

44

early days we'd just go shopping wherever we'd travel, like any popstar. There were many things you could only buy in Milan or Tokyo or New York then. You could only get Emporio Armani in Milan – amazing! The first time we went to Milan, in January 1986, there was this huge, huge painted billboard of a guy in a grey coat. We loved it all. In Japan we'd look for Issey Miyake and this Japanese label Poshboy. Really amazing. The long black linen coat I wore for the early videos came from Eric Watson, the photographer.

GJ: You borrowed his coat?

NT: He had one that looked great on me so I bought my own, from Stephen Linard. Beautiful coat – I could wear it now, still. It was the perfect cut. It looked great with a white shirt and tie, or no tie. You don't wear a severe black coat like that with the top button of your shirt not done up. You'd look stupid.

GJ: Do you still have the coat?

NT: I think I do, but I don't know where – must be somewhere in my basement, together with the Jil Sander suits and the Miyakes.

GJ: Was there a mod thing about the buttoning up? I mean, Ray Davies kind of invented the look in my opinion.

NT: I never thought about that, but subconsciously I probably did.

GJ: There was mod, and then in the '80s, after punk, music cleaned up and electronified, and so did the looks. Bands started to look like art school students. Joy Division…

NT: True, very buttoned up. I was also very much into that Echo & the Bunnymen look of a buttoned-up shirt and a dark-green raincoat. I always liked that look.

GJ: At one of the first photo shoots with the Pet Shop Boys you're both wearing preppy polo shirts.

NT: That's our 'casuals' look. The 'casuals' was sort of a post-mod movement in London around '82, '83, maybe through '84. It was when trainers came in and people started wearing expensive sports shirts from Sergio Tacchini and Lacoste. You wouldn't really go to East London back then, but there was one club in Bethnal Green, Benjy's, which was this gay club where the entire crowd were 'casuals' – East End boys in ice-blue jeans, trainers and Lacoste, dancing on classic hi-energy.

GJ: Sounds amazing.

NT: I loved it. The first time I bought a Lacoste shirt I couldn't believe how expensive it was! Also, when Chris and I went to New York we came back with Nike trainers and cagoules – very early hip-hop. In those days going to Foot Locker was exciting.

GJ: What are cagoules?

NT: They're like anoraks. They had silver lining and we'd wear them over a Lacoste shirt or Fred Perry, Lonsdale. Chris brought a tennis racket to one of our first photo shoots. He's wearing these tight bleached jeans with a white Sergio Tacchini shirt and a tennis racket. I'm wearing a dark blue polo shirt.

GJ: But soon you started to look much more formal.

NT: The Pet Shop Boys thing, as it developed, became 'Neil is formal, Chris is street'. It didn't take long to figure that out, because that's what we're like. Chris doesn't like wearing formal shoes, he likes wearing trainers. I still feel funny wearing trainers. Every now and then I get a pair of running shoes that I like.

GJ: Women's shoes? Did you say women's shoes?

NT: Women's shoes? Running shoes! But it's funny to say that, because it's so common for me to see a nice pair of boots in the shop, I point at them and they say, 'They're women's, sir.' Why is that? Why do women get the best bloody boots? They do, you know?

GJ: Is there a distinct moment in the history of the Pet Shop Boys where you went from looking quite normal and dressed up to wearing costumes and disguises such as the pointy hats?

NT: We started doing disguises and costumes when… Well, I would say we always did a bit of costume. Even the long black linen coat was a costume, you know? I wouldn't have worn that on the street. If I had worn that in public I would think that I was trying to look like me. That coat was in two videos, so we got our money's worth out of it, but otherwise I wouldn't wear it.

GJ: Do you make sure you're properly dressed whenever you pop out to get a pint of milk, just in case somebody would spot you?

NT: I don't. Firstly, I always walk down the back of the King's Road and then appear at the right spot – I wouldn't take the main road per se. And secondly London's not really bad for paparazzi – it's not like Berlin, where it's a nightmare. We recorded our latest album in LA – LA is very paparazzi, obviously.

GJ: LA must be terrible in terms of paparazzi.

NT: Yes. You actually can't go to Rodeo Drive.
I hate paparazzi, it's stupid, really. We
watched this film about Ron Galella, who
stalked Jackie Onassis for decades and
basically ruined her life, and now
there's some naff art gallery saying that
it's art.

GJ: Do you know if your phone was hacked in
the great British phone hacking scandal?

NT: I don't think I was. We're not celebrity
enough, we're not Robbie Williams or Elton,
who doesn't even have a phone – he uses his
bodyguard's. But what I don't understand in
the fuss about hacking voicemails is: who still
uses voicemail? Do you have a lot of
voicemail messages?

GJ: I don't.

NT: Exactly, and neither do I. Who phones you
up and, when you don't pick up, leaves
a message with embarrassing details about

their sex life or something? Nobody does that. But what about text message hacking or e-mail hacking? That'd be much more interesting for the press and I don't believe it doesn't happen. But I don't think we can face the drama of an investigation into e-mail hacking yet.

GJ: God, yes, imagine… I wanted to ask you about this broad-shouldered black suit with a white buttoned-up shirt that you're wearing in the video for 'So Hard'.

NT: I call that the 'Iranian' look. It's Thierry Mugler. 1990. I think I'm wearing it in the 'Being Boring' video too. The jacket literally had *this* extra space. You'd feel like a fool if you'd wear it now. As David Bowie said so rightly, 'Padded shoulders are the flares of the '80s.' It was the same silhouette but upside down. I had about one year of wearing Mugler – I had to stop wearing it because George Michael started wearing it.

GJ: There's one interesting theory about

buttoning up: that it's the most rebellious thing to do as it deliberately leaves out the tie. With an open shirt, one wouldn't question where the tie went, but with a buttoned-up shirt the big question is: where's the tie?

NT: I quite like ties too. But I agree, wearing no tie is sort of sexy because you know the turmoil that's going on beneath it. The repressiveness of it is sort of sexy. I've always quite liked that Iranian look – black suit, white shirt, no tie. Maybe it's a religious thing? Also, a shirt that's unbuttoned reminds me of the '60s and '70s when people were showing off their hairy chests and gold chains. I don't know… I think you also have to have the right neck to do things like that.

GJ: You're saying the act of buttoning up also has its physical roots?

NT: Of course. If I had a thick neck we'd be having a completely different conversation.

52

Dior Homme by Hedi Slimane, Spring 2007 campaign,
photographed by Hedi Slimane.

Fashionable Ways

Alexander Fury on the odd existence of the buttoned-up shirt in fashion

Blue collar, white collar, starchy, buttoned up – am I talking about a lad, or a laundromat? Could be both, but truth be told you don't think of clothes when you hear those words, you think of people. The language of clothes is persuasive, and all-pervasive – so much so that it's become part of our everyday vernacular. 'Clothes maketh the man,' as the hackneyed half-baked quote goes, but perhaps we don't realize quite how fashioned our male is these days. There's a striking moment in *American Psycho*, Bret Easton Ellis' parable of '80s excess, where the anti-hero Patrick Bateman unfastens his shirt collar in a crowded downtown New York City nightclub, yet is perplexed that he's still rumbled as the quintessential yuppie. In Mr Bateman's eyes, the unfastening of a single button could magically transmogrify him from establishment to rebel.

So how much significance can we ascribe to the buttoning and unbuttoning of a collar? In fashion circles, it's equivalent to a tectonic shift: it may seem small, but it often ricochets off the Richter scale. Look at the lean, mean menswear silhouette Hedi Slimane introduced during his tenure at Dior Homme. At the time, it seemed revolutionary, but it was actually about precision, about the importance ascribed to the tiniest of details. Slimane slimmed: seams pinched in by an extra millimetre, trousers tapered and cropped at the ankle, and those shirt collars precisely buttoned to streamline his silhouettes.

How much of it was fashion and how much style? After all, they are two very different things. You can categorize the former as the clothes you wear on your back, the latter as the way you put them on. Fashion and style are also verbs: to fashion is to make; to style (at least in the modern sense) is to tinker with something that already exists to make it look new. I said the two were very different, but they certainly aren't mutually exclusive. Indeed, if we take Patrick Bateman's opened collar as a symbol of fashionable rebellion, it can be said that by the end of the '90s the opposite would be true: the unfastened collar became a mark of fashion.

In October 1996, Gucci's designer Tom Ford was in the process of jump-starting the Italian leather-goods brand's fashion appeal for the masses. He did it by shock, and by sex. That season, in Gucci's Spring/Summer 1997 fashion show, the shirts on Mr Ford's male models were unbuttoned to the waist, clinging on for dear life – mere accessories to acres of waxed chest streaked with grease. Collars were vestigial: it was important that they existed, but they served no real function. That is now a lifetime ago in fashion years, light years away from today – the wrenched-open shirt collar was the hallmark of Ford's first five years at the fashion frontline. He sported the look himself: one too many shirt-buttons unfastened, an inch too much chest hair on show. One could throw out tired, trite references to snake-hipped '70s lotharios in descriptions of Ford's fellows. It may be clichéd, but it has a ring of truth: Ford relived his own misbegotten youth in the guise of his Gucci guys – a youth he himself admitted was spent writhing on the floor of Californian condos in various states of fashionable undress.

But Tom Ford's vision, of course, wasn't the only one to mark fashion in the 1990s. Raf Simons, the Belgian menswear revolutionary, was undoubtedly more experimental, exploring rebellion and formalizing styles hitherto only seen in mosh pits and on street corners. Miuccia Prada can be credited as more technologically advanced, pushing men into synthetic fibres that managed to speak simultaneously of a utilitarian future and a past in questionable taste. However, Ford's Gucci probably clothed more men, especially as most men aren't looking for fashions that challenge. Mr Ford's fashions were an exercise in unabashed nostalgia, those open collars an open door to his customers to experience Ford's fantasy of the '70s. That's the crux of what Ford was selling: sex, or at least its salacious connotations. And men were buying into it.

It's silly to believe all that salaciousness stopped at the end of the '90s. Even today, the nadir of Eurotrash flash decrees a gaping gash at the collar, preferably with flesh bared neck-to-navel. It's ubiquitous around the Mediterranean and virtually a national costume in Italy. In France, the media-savvy philosopher and politician Bernard-Henri Lévy is as widely known for his hysterical open collars as for his polemic. But fashion, on the whole, has moved on. Even Tom Ford has shifted his allegiances: back in 2002, he offered a collection of arch, starched wing-collared evening shirts fastened high on the neck. Granted, there was nary a tie amongst his boys. Ford has confessed, 'I wear my shirts open because ties give me a headache… I start to get a migraine.' (However, when he launched his eponymous 'Tom Ford' brand, five years later, it was suit, shirt *and* tie galore.)

Talking about moving on, it was the 'experimental' likes of Prada and Raf Simons (both under his own name and latterly for Jil Sander, where he was incidentally installed under the auspices of Prada) who were to ring in the changes in men's fashion for the next decade. That's not to denigrate Mr Ford's Gucci coup: it's just that fashion always reacts against that what's gone before. If it's not new, it's at least different.

Look at the way Miuccia Prada occasionally deals with shirt buttons: she shifts the buttons from the front to the back of the shirt. It is a simple conceit, effectively reversing the shirt, leaving the front of the garment unadorned. But this is more than mere surface play. The mechanics of a back-buttoning shirt hark back to a different time, and to a different sex. A woman is buttoned into her clothes; a man buttons himself into his. At least, that's what convention has told us since the mid-19th century, the last time the true gentleman didn't dress, but was 'dressed' by his valet.

The rear-fastening shirts I'm thinking of first

59

Text continues on page 68

14-year-old Felix Howard, styled by Ray Petri and photographed by Jamie Morgan of the influential Buffalo movement, 1987.

Raf Simons x Fred Perry campaign image, from 2009.
Photograph by Willy Vanderperre, styling by Olivier Rizzo.

A gentleman on the street in Florence, Italy, photographed
by Scott Schuman, also known as The Sartorialist, in 2012.

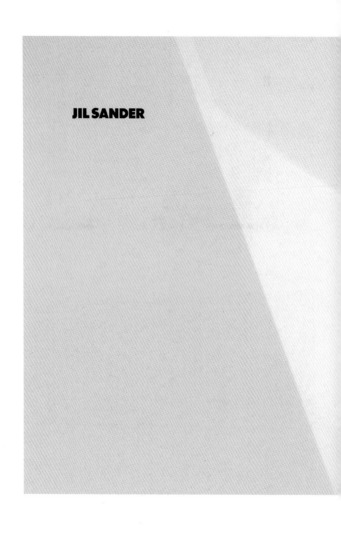

Jil Sander campaign from Spring 2007, when Raf Simons designed the collection. Photograph by Willy Vanderperre, styling by Olivier Rizzo.

The American fashion designer Thom Browne,
photographed by Marcelo Krasilcic for the debut issue of
Fantastic Man, 2005.

An androgynous look styled by Joe McKenna and
photographed by Alasdair McLellan for *i-D* magazine, 2008.

Film director David Lynch notoriously wears his shirts
buttoned up; here in a photograph by Kiino Viland.

and foremost belong to Prada's Autumn/Winter 2008 collection. The fashion journalist Tim Blanks of *style.com* dubbed it 'Beau du Jour', a sly reference not only to Luis Buñuel's 1967 BDSM cult film *Belle du Jour*, but also to Beau Brummell, precisely the type of dandy for whom a valet was a necessity rather than a luxury. Brummell made his appearance his very identity but, paradoxically, demanded absolute anonymity from his attire. If John Bull turns to look at you in the street, you are not well dressed – this was Mr Brummell's maxim, which became a mantra for a century of menswear. In retrospect it was pithily dubbed 'The Great Masculine Renunciation', a blanket term for eschewing extravagance in dress for a sober costume of navy, black and incandescent white that occurred after the Industrial Revolution. White was Brummell's leitmotif: a mania for cleanliness manifested in snowy, starchy cravats folded and wrapped around the neck to form a pedestal upon which the head could nobly repose – not a mile away from the contemporary stayed and still-starched shirt collar.

But back to Prada: when Mrs Prada skews her fastenings to the back, she's rendering man subservient, wilfully so. She does it quite often – for Autumn/Winter 2011, she offered what the Prada press office euphemistically described as 'a back-buttoning silk-georgette shirt in pale blue' – imagine a big girl's blouse. The idea of Prada's men being buttoned into their clothes evokes not the moneyed grandeur of the gentleman, but something slightly seedier – a kept boy, perhaps, dressed and undressed at the whim of a benefactor. Or maybe just a boy dressed by a doting mother.

That's another kick to the tightly buttoned collar – it synchs with fashion's fixation on youth. Male models aren't men anymore, they're teenage boys. But while it's quite common to see boys dressed up as grown-up men, the opposite becomes interestingly perverse: to dress up men as children. That's what Raf Simons tackles season after season, taking as his inspirations school uniform and teenage rebellion, conformity and its antithesis. Youth is omnipotent, and if the '90s offered a shirt unbuttoned over the swelled chest of an adult, Simons buttons his shirt tight across the concave sternum of a child. That's no criticism, just an observation.

'Elegance is the new sex,' said Tom Ford to Suzy Menkes of the *International Herald Tribune* when he showed a collection featuring starched evening shirts back in 2002. But sex is out of the equation when it comes to Raf Simons' vision of the buttoned collar. The fastened collar represents control; it's emblematic of chastity, like a country vicar tightly fastened into his clerical best. It is a symbol of conformity, characteristic of the uniform Simons is so impassioned of. But you also think of mods, skinheads and casuals, the counter-culture movements who harnessed the pin-neat pinned collar as a mask. (Mr Simons also designs a range for the British sportswear brand Fred Perry, whose signature cotton piqué polo shirts are beloved on football terraces and at scooter rallies alike.) In England, a colloquial term for angry is 'shirty'. It always feels especially apt at a Raf Simons show, tension barely concealed beneath a tightly buttoned collar.

The new element added to the mix in 21st-century menswear is a relaxing of the rules of dressing. It's not about casual, dress-down culture: in fact, it's the exact opposite. 'In all the collections I have created there has always been the mix of formal and informal, sports and suits. I have always encouraged breaking with formality,' says Lucas Ossendrijver, the authoritative menswear director at Lanvin. Rather than breaking with formality, however, Ossendrijver's work can be credited as part of a movement to break down the boundaries between casual and formal. At Lanvin, an evening suit may be cut from sweatshirt fabric, a T-shirt from hammered silk. Shirt collars are made of grosgrain ribbon, irrespective of whether the garment they are attached to is a cotton lawn dress shirt or a waffle-knit tennis shirt. 'I always envisaged pushing the rules of dressing for men,' says Ossendrijver. 'For me it was all about blurring the lines. We have never separated, always integrated the sports and formal elements to make one fluid collection.'

In a fashion landscape already preoccupied with casual, Ossendrijver's Lanvin legacy is to give formality a new relevance – his relaxed, modern variant on staples of formalwear are translated into styles men can wear everyday. The most visible manifestation of that new formality is those tightly fastened collars.

'New'. That's a key word in fashion – even if it's just the idea rather than the actuality. Fashion historian and theorist professor Ulrich Lehmann has stated that 'in order to become the new, fashion always cites the old,' that it is merely the juxtaposition of idea against idea that creates the impression of novelty. A 'fashion' is only new next to that what has just ceased to be fashionable. The terribly proper and almost-prim buttoned collars at first seemed alien next to Gucci's slashed neckline, which itself was a glamour-sated reaction against grunge, which came bang on the end of Patrick Bateman's pre-crash yuppie excess. And that's sort of what fashion is all about.

Construction

Variations of collars, photographed by
Jop van Bennekom

A classic standard or house
collar on a Lanvin shirt.

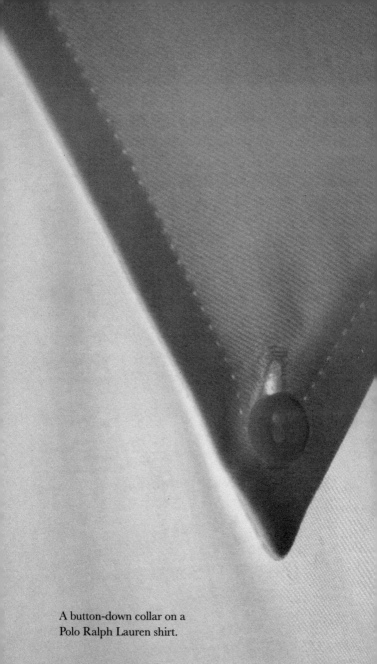

A button-down collar on a
Polo Ralph Lauren shirt.

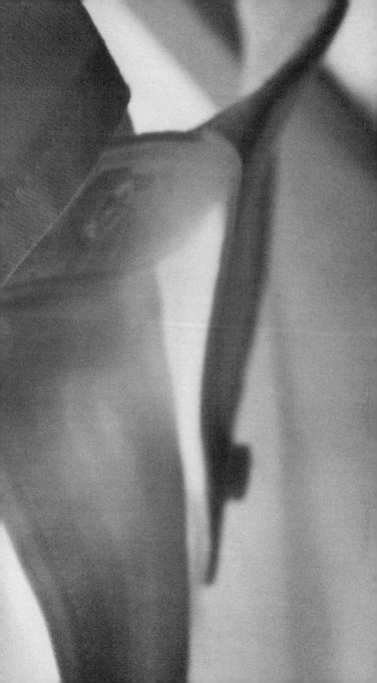

A sharp-point collar on a
Jil Sander shirt.

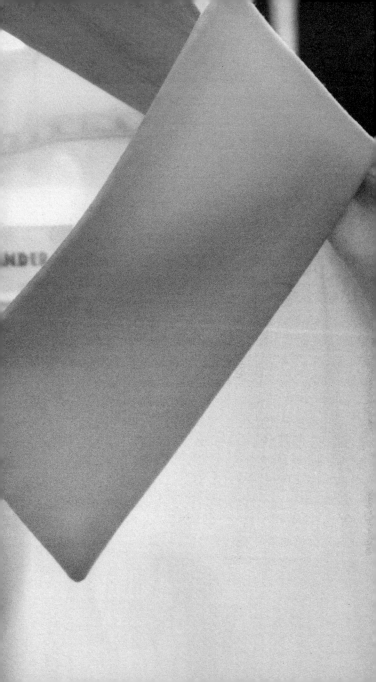

A two-penny round collar on
a Brooks Brothers shirt.

Simon Topping was lead singer of A Certain Ratio until 1983. Photo by David Corio.

Repression

Simon Reynolds on music, masochism and the
strict style of mod men

The connection between Englishness, violence
and style is the essence of mod – the youth
rage that swept over Britain from the late
1950s until the mid 1960s and has remained
present ever since. Mods were famous, or
infamous, for violence. They warred with their
enemies, the rockers, in ritualized battles on
the beaches of Brighton, Margate, Broadstairs,
Clacton and Bournemouth. The antagonism
was characterized by an almost jihad-like
zeal. Mods despised rockers as their spiritual
antithesis – dirty and lumpen where the mods
were clean and aspirational. Rockers saw mods,

some of whom wore eye make-up, as effeminate and stuck up. Mods were city kids who looked to Europe for style; the rockers were from the countryside and looked to America. Mods rode to battle in phalanxes of dainty streamlined Italian scooters; the rockers arrived on big noisy motorbikes, as greasy as their Brylcreemed hair.

The violence of the mods as they rampaged against the rockers was, on one level, simply righteous disgust for their abject opposite. But mod style itself could be seen as having an inherent undercurrent of violence. First, there was the symbolic violence of dressing sharper than your social superiors ('powerful people – businessmen in suits, take their clothes, retain your identity' as Ian Page of mod revival band Secret Affair put it). But also a kind of imploded violence: the neurotic fastidiousness of dress and grooming was a sort of voluntarily worn straitjacket, a near-masochistic set of constraints and rules.

Partially it was a reaction to Britain's existing class structure, over which the individual had no control and into which he was inserted.

Mods displaced and exceeded this by an invented and freely chosen class system based on style: one that allowed for even greater snobbery, a superiority complex founded on esoteric knowledge and the mastery of subtle stylistic rules that changed by the week.

Kevin Pearce, the music journalist and author, wrote that mods 'had to be the first to hear something, own something, know something, wear something, be something, do something, and then move on … Mod styling was about precision … Everything had to be just so. Inordinate attention was paid to detail.' Mods wore their shirts smartly buttoned up. They rebelled not through informality but through inventing even stricter rules than people conventionally obeyed in terms of clothing and grooming. This stringent regime, stoked and sharpened by amphetamines, demanded some kind of release, a breaking free. That could take the form of mayhem (as with the war with the rockers) or through theatricalized disorder. Which is where The Who came in; a band designed by mod philosopher Pete Meaden, the group's manager in their early days. Meaden deliberately shaped The Who to appeal to the existing mod subculture, which until then had been based not around following bands but dancing to imported soul and R&B records.

The Who's sound was white R&B so amped-up and amphetamine-uptight it came apart at the seams: Keith Moon's free-flailing cymbal crashes and tom rolls, Pete Townshend's slashed and scything power chords, John Entwhistle's bass lunges. A sound expressive not of sexual desire, but of an unrest at once social and existential. Mod was fundamentally asexual: as Pearce notes, mods 'simply were not interested. They were... too self-absorbed ... Mods were free, clear of emotional ties. They rejected peer pressure to pair off.' The boys dressed and danced to impress other boys, not to attract girls. Drugs also had something to do with it, suppressing sex drive along with other needs and appetites (such as food and sleep). Speed created a sexless intensity, a plateau state of arrested orgasm that the mods, revealingly, called 'blocked'.

The pent-up pressure had to blow somehow, though, and mod's latent violence was dramatized by Moon and Townshend in their climactic orgies of instrument-smashing: supposedly inspired by art-school student Townsend's encounter with Gustav Metzger's auto-destructive art, but really the orgasmic release that mod music, mod psychology, mod neurology urgently required.

In the immediate aftermath of 'My Generation', 'I Can't Explain', 'Anyway Anyhow Anywhere', and the other early Who singles, young bands like The Eyes, The Creation and John's Children picked up on the band's loudness and distortion and in 1966–7 recorded a series of singles that fans and collectors subsequently have come to call 'freakbeat': mod tipping into a jagged, edge-of-chaos frenzy under the influence of speed and LSD. The strange blend of menace and feyness in songs like The Eyes' 'When The Night Falls' and 'My Degeneration' or John's Children's 'A Midsummer Night's Scene' and 'Desdemona' simmered with a spontaneous combustibility that was uniquely English, rooted in the characteristic native psychology of neurotic uptightness and lashing-out rage.

With this came a deliberately unrelaxed, non-casual mode of dress that crystallized something essential about mod: the buttoned-up look. ('Buttoned up', or its equivalent 'bottled up', could almost be the definition of Englishness.) It's a fashion move that involves the fastening of the top button on a shirt, but the absence of a tie. Buttoned up, or the 'air tie', is something that one can see in numerous photographs of The Who, The Eyes and The Creation.

Buttoned up is smarter and more formal than having the shirt loose at the top, but the absence of a tie is a glaring and pointed gesture. It indicates that you're not headed for a conventional workplace, but that neither are you dressing sloppy (as with the classic image of the office worker, arriving at home or in the pub, finally free to loosen his tie). 'Buttoned up' does not necessarily define mod, but it

87

Text continues on page 96

Mod superstars The Who in an image from 1967. From left to right: Keith Moon, Pete Townshend, Roger Daltrey and John Entwistle.

Singer Paul Haig of the Scottish post-punk band Josef K,
photographed by Harry Papadopoulos, 1980.

Singer and frontman Robert Smith of The Cure,
photographed by Derek W. Ridgers in 1989.

Singer Jim Reid formed The Jesus and Mary Chain together
with his brother William in 1983.

Singer and guitarist Glenn Mercer of The Feelies from New Jersey, USA, photographed in 1980 by Joe Stevens.

Billy Hassett, singer of mod-revival group The Chords from London, photographed by Kevin Cummins in the late 1970s.

Scottish post-punk band Orange Juice photographed by
Chris Craymer, 1982.

Singer Bob Manton of mod-revivalists Purple Hearts from Romford, photographed by Jill Furmanovsky in 1979.

nonetheless feels like a quintessentially mod mannerism.

A variant of this throat-constricting look continued with those 'hard mods', the skinheads, and their love of the tennis shirts made by Fred Perry and Ben Sherman, which, whether long-sleeve or short-sleeve, were almost invariably worn buttoned up. Unfairly or not, skinheads were synonymous in the public imagination with violence, as the media stoked their folk-devil image as prolier-than-thou 'bovver boys' who brutalized hippies (hated for their long hair and dirtiness) and Asian immigrants (but not West Indians, whom the skins admired and emulated for their short hair and slick clothing, and whose high-energy ska rhythms they danced to).

Interestingly, during the 1970s the mod or buttoned-up look gradually lost its association with physical violence and became cerebral. The neat-freak neurosis and Englishness remained but mod as an ongoing tradition became more about a severity of *mind*: the stark separation of oneself from the lumpen, the vulgar, the commonplace. It was an influence on English punk (the Sex Pistols covered Who songs) but the two class-of-'77 bands who owed most to mod were The Jam and Subway Sect.

Paul Weller and Vic Godard, leaders and frontmen of The Jam and Subway Sect respectively, emerged from what I call the liminal class, a blurry zone where upper working class bleeds into the lower middle class. This shaky social stratum is where so much of Britain's musical creativity and distinctive national pop character stems from.

The precariousness of the liminal class makes it a fertile breeding ground for a psychology of quest and mission. They're usually white collar and typically clerical workers who felt superior to lumpen manual workers, yet were rarely destined for higher education, and therefore resentful of the college-bound, privately educated upper middle class. The hallmark of the mindset is a kind of aesthetic moralism, an absolutist view that is binary and polarizing in its division of the world into the righteous and the square, the hip and the hapless. Or as

Weller put it in 'Start!', a song about the fleeting joy of meeting a soul brother: 'Knowing that someone in this world/Loves with a passion called hate.' It's an English archetype: young men, chips on both shoulders, burning with a peculiarly sour ardour, chasing a purity and truth beyond the fate of mundanity and mediocrity otherwise mapped out for them, finding transcendence in a pair of shoes or a 7-inch soul single.

The sound of The Jam and Subway Sect is rooted in that mod/freakbeat sound of wiry fractious guitars and nervous tension; a version of R&B that wants to explode every-which-way rather than groove. A totally English sound, now curiously inflected with an explicit anti-Americanism. (African-American music is exempted from this of course, as is New York: The Velvet Underground, The Voidoids and Television were touchstones for Subway Sect.) Vic Godard deliberately purged his lyrics of Americanisms and told me that early on the Subway Sect played a song called 'US Cunts'. In true mod style he looked to Europe: particularly to France (he admired the philosopher and writer Théophile Gautier and the composer Claude Debussy, even playing the latter's music as warm-up before the group came onstage) but also, as if propelled further eastwards by his anti-Americanism, developing a love of the Eastern Bloc countries. Despite being one of the UK's biggest groups of the new wave era, The Jam totally – and revealingly – failed to make it in America (unlike the more rock 'n' roll Clash). Weller professed to be not much concerned about breaking the US market.

In an early '80s interview, Weller contrasted what he thought were stylish and square: in the negative category were concepts like 'dirty, rock 'n' roll, rock, out of it,' while in the positive list were 'clean, keeping straight, cappuccino, soul, Europe, classical, symmetry.' (An obsession with cleanliness and keeping up respectable appearances is a hallmark of the British working class: hence the folk image of the housewife on her knees ferociously scrubbing the doorstep until it gleams.)

The Jam and Subway Sect both proved

highly influential, each in their own different way disseminating the mod ideal. Weller's progeny was more literal-minded: the mod revival of 1979–80, a horde of bands mostly from the east and south zones of outer London, towns like Walthamstow and Romford and Merton. Secret Affair wore real ties not air ties. They aimed to start their own youth momevent called Glory Boys. And when nouveau mods started turning up to their gigs, Secret Affair found themselves anointed the leaders of the revivalist scene. For singer and spokesmen Ian Page, mod was all about triumph over your social superiors through style and superciliousness: 'I can cut you down by combing my hair/Nothing touches a Glory Boy.' Or as he phrased it in a 'New Mod Manifesto' penned for *Sounds* magazine: 'a moment's intensity – young man, sharp look, street corner, a cold stare from old eyes in a young face. Pride/dignity – self respect.'

Lurking just below the surface pride and positivism was tremendous bitterness. In a striking metaphor, Purple Hearts'

'Frustration' connects feelings of entrapment with the very clothes meant to signify triumph through style: 'I get frustration/I wear it like a suit/But the jacket fits too tightly/And there's lead inside my boots.' If you look on YouTube for that other mod revival anthem 'The British Way of Life' by The Chords, you'll find that some fan has constructed their own video for this song of oddly uplifting despair with vintage footage of violence and public disorder from British TV news: '80s street riots, football hooligans running amok, protesters hurling Molotov cocktails, striking workers battling the police...

One could say that the USA is, by and large, a looser and louder culture than Britain, and one that is perfectly capable of both rowdiness and extreme violence (from serial killers to political assassins to mass shooters, as well as ethnic strife and mob behaviour). But it's England that invented hooliganism and style-tribe warfare. There is no other country in the world where young people have beaten the crap out of each other for no reason beyond differences in sports allegiance, clothing and music taste.

The Jam's legions of imitators were centred around London and its surrounding counties. Subway Sect, for some reason, had a particularly strong impact in the North and above all in Scotland. Vic Godard was a cult figure to post-punk groups like Orange Juice and Josef K, who admired Subway Sect's angular guitars and sharp yet subdued image and who picked up on Godard's 'we oppose all rock 'n' roll rhetoric.' Both groups went in for the buttoned-up look in a big way, but Josef K went further by wearing suits too. 'I was interested in the original mod movement,' recalled Josef K's guitarist Malcolm Ross. 'That was one of the influences in wearing suits... I wanted some kind of dignity.' Wired and wiry, Josef K's sound crackled with nervous energy and was about as far from groovy or let-it-all-hang-out as you could get. 'We didn't smoke dope in Josef K,' said Ross. 'Speed was acceptable – similar to the mod thing of being in control and alert. Being drunk or stoned wasn't cool. But speeding a bit was okay.' Orange Juice likewise espoused an anti-rock 'n' roll ethos that verged on prudish: no alcohol, no groupies or sleeping around. Sex only if you were properly in love. It led to *Sounds* journalist Dave McCullough dubbing them and the other bands on Glasgow's Postcard Records label as 'New Puritans'.

In subsequent decades from their clothes to their sound to their attitude and demeanour, Orange Juice and Josef K represented the transition from post-punk to indiepop, a process that was continued and completed by other Scottish groups like The Happy Family, The Jesus and Mary Chain, The Jasmine Minks and Primal Scream. Mod was part of the DNA: Alan McGee christened his label Creation (home for The Jesus and Mary Chain, the Minks and the Scream) while his own band Biff Bang Pow! was named after one of The Creation's singles. In subsequent decades, mod-ishness, and in particular the buttoned-up look, has become part of indiepop's make-up, surfacing repeatedly with groups like Hatcham Social, A Certain Ratio, The Housemartins and The Pastels. But along the way the aggression faded away completely, to be replaced by apartness: the look now signified fragility, unworldliness, not being of-this-time.

Junction No. 5:
Wilton Way, E8

Junction No. 6:
Fleur De Lis Street and Blossom Street, E1

Credits

Fantastic Man is the biannual journal for the modern man. Founded in Amsterdam, the Netherlands, in 2005, the magazine is published in English and distributed internationally.

Buttoned-Up:
Edited by Gert Jonkers and Jop van Bennekom

Editorial assistance by Matthew Lowe, Andrew T. Vottero and Sebastiaan Groenen

Design assistance by Merel van den Berg

With contributions by Jodie Barnes, Paul Flynn, Alexander Fury, Benjamin Alexander Huseby, Isaac Lock, Matt Mulhall, Owen Myers and Simon Reynolds

Thanks to Magnus Åkesson, Giordano Cioni, Shaun Cole, Kacper Lasota, Alex LeRose, Alex Needham, *NME* magazine, Richard O'Mahony and Rosco Production

Boys
Photography by Benjamin Alexander Huseby
Styling by Jodie Barnes
Grooming by Matt Mulhall at Streeters London
Photographic assistance by Tanya Houghton
Styling assistance by Andrew T. Vottero and
Camilla Holmes
Production by Giordano Cioni at Rosco Production
Models: Joshua Aberhart, Giordano Cioni, Abel Llavall-
Ubach, Moses Manley, Owen Myers, Jasper Toron
Nielsen, Matthew Vant

p.5   Giordano is wearing a light-blue Oxford shirt by
       Polo Ralph Lauren with a brown herringbone
       jacket by Dunhill.

pp.   Joshua is wearing a green gingham shirt by Polo
20–21 Ralph Lauren with a grey herringbone jacket by
       Margaret Howell.

p.22   Moses is wearing a light-green Oxford shirt with a
       brown-and-white check tweed jacket, both by Polo
       Ralph Lauren.

p.23   Owen is wearing a light-blue-and-white check shirt
       by Dunhill with an olive-green jacket by Margaret
       Howell.

pp.   Abel is wearing a blue chambray shirt by Margaret
24–25 Howell with a brown-and-white herringbone tweed
      jacket by Polo Ralph Lauren.

p.26   Matthew is wearing a grey-and-white micro-check
      shirt by Margaret Howell with a green-and-beige
      jacket by Polo Ralph Lauren.

p.27   Jasper is wearing a purple-and-red-and-white check
      shirt by Polo Ralph Lauren with a camel jacket by
      Hackett London.

Fashionable Ways
Images on pages 53 and 67 copyright Trunk Archive.
Image on page 62 copyright Scott Schuman.

Construction
Photography by Jop van Bennekom
Styling by Andrew T. Vottero

Repression
Images on pages 81 and 88–95 courtesy of *NME*
magazine's photo archive, London.

PENGUIN LINES

Choose Your Journey

If you're looking for...

Romantic Encounters

Heads and Straights
by Lucy Wadham
(the Circle line)

Waterloo–City, City–Waterloo
by Leanne Shapton
(the Waterloo & City line)

Tales of Growing Up and Moving On

Heads and Straights
by Lucy Wadham
(the Circle line)

A Good Parcel of English Soil
by Richard Mabey
(the Metropolitan line)

Mind the Child
by Camila Batmanghelidjh and
Kids Company
(the Victoria line)

The 32 Stops
by Danny Dorling
(the Central line)

A History of Capitalism
According to the Jubilee Line
by John O'Farrell
(the Jubilee line)

A Northern Line Minute
by William Leith
(the Northern line)

Mind the Child
by Camila Batmanghelidjh and
Kids Company
(the Victoria line)

Heads and Straights
by Lucy Wadham
(the Circle line)

Laughter and Tears

Breaking Boundaries

Drift
by Philippe Parreno
(the Hammersmith & City line)

Buttoned-Up
by Fantastic Man
(the East London line)

Waterloo–City, City–Waterloo
by Leanne Shapton
(the Waterloo & City line)

Earthbound
by Paul Morley
(the Bakerloo line)

Mind the Child
by Camila Batmanghelidjh
and Kids Company
(the Victoria line)

The Blue Riband
by Peter York
(the Piccadilly line)

**A Bit of
Politics**

The 32 Stops
by Danny Dorling
(the Central line)

*A History of Capitalism
According to the Jubilee Line*
by John O'Farrell
(the Jubilee line)

**Musical
Direction**

Heads and Straights
by Lucy Wadham
(the Circle line)

Earthbound
by Paul Morley
(the Bakerloo line)

The Blue Riband
by Peter York
(the Piccadilly line)

**Tube
Knowledge**

*What We Talk About When
We Talk About The Tube*
by John Lanchester
(the District line)

*A Good Parcel of
English Soil*
by Richard Mabey
(the Metropolitan line)

**A Breath of
Fresh Air**

*A Good Parcel of
English Soil*
by Richard Mabey
(the Metropolitan line)

**Design for
Life**

Waterloo–City, City–Waterloo
by Leanne Shapton
(the Waterloo & City line)

Buttoned-Up
by Fantastic Man
(the East London line)

Drift
by Philippe Parreno
(the Hammersmith & City line)